Plan
Prepare
COOK

D0231894

A Tasty Main Meal

Rita Storey

W
FRANKLIN WATTS
LONDON • SYDNEY

Contents

Franklin Watts
338 Euston Road
London NW1 3BH

Franklin Watts Australia
Level 17/207 Kent Street
Sydney NSW 2000

This edition © Franklin Watts 2014

Series editor: Sarah Peutrill
Art director: Jonathan Hair

Series designed and created for Franklin Watts
by Storeybooks
Designer: Rita Storey
Editor: Nicola Barber
Photography: Tudor Photography

A CIP catalogue record for this book is available
from the British Library

Printed in China

Dewey classification: 641.5'2

ISBN: 978 1 4451 2982 2

Picture credits
All photographs Tudor Photography, Banbury
unless otherwise stated. Shutterstock p5;
Wishlistimages.co.uk p4

Cover images Tudor Photography
All photos posed by models. Thanks to Jack Abbott,
Amy Mobley, Serish Begum and Jordan McElavaine.

Franklin Watts is a division of Hachette Children's
Books, an Hachette UK company
www.hachette.co.uk

Pages marked with ⬇ have a related free downloadable activity sheet at www.franklinwatts/downloads. Find out more on page 32.

Words in **bold** are in the glossary on page 30.

Before you start

- Wash your hands before and after preparing food.
- Ask an adult to help when the recipe uses the cooker or grill.
- If you have long hair, clip or tie it back.
- Dry your hands before you plug in or unplug any electrical appliances.
- Wear an apron or an old shirt.
- Wash up as you go along.
- Be extra careful with sharp knives.
- Ask an adult to help with the liquidiser/food processor.
- Ask an adult to help you weigh the ingredients.

Look out for this useful guide to each recipe.

How long each recipe takes to make.

How difficult each recipe is to make.

If the food needs to be cooked.

For most people the main meal of the day is eaten in the evening. This is usually when school and work are finished and there is time to prepare and cook a meal.

Fast food

Supermarkets sell a wide variety of ready-prepared meals. This 'fast food' may be high in sugar and **fat**. It also often contains **artificial**

Starchy foods

You should eat **starchy** foods every day – they should make up about a third of what you eat in a day. A portion of potatoes, pasta or rice is a good idea as part of a main meal.
- Choose **wholegrain** or **wholewheat** varieties.

Meat, fish, chicken, eggs and beans

These foods contain **protein**. Meat, fish and eggs are often the basis of a main meal. Beans also contain protein, and they can replace meat or fish in the main meals of **vegetarians**.

colourings and **flavourings**, as well as **preservatives**. Try not to eat this type of **processed food** too often.

If you are in a hurry, cooking a bowl of pasta with a delicious sauce can be just as fast as heating up a ready-prepared meal. It will taste great and is healthy too.

The recipes in this book are quick and easy. Knowing that you have prepared and cooked them yourself is really satisfying.

Why we eat

The human body is like a machine that needs **energy** to work. Energy is released from the food you eat and used up by your body.

A healthy balance

To be healthy you must eat enough food to produce the energy needed by your body. But if you eat more food than your body actually requires, it is turned into fat. If you do this all the time, you keep getting fatter.

When you **exercise** you use up energy from the food you have eaten.

Fruit and vegetables

You should eat at least five portions of fruit and vegetables every day (5-a-day). A portion of fruit or vegetables is about 80 g (3 oz), or roughly one handful. Fruit and vegetables should make up about a third of what you eat in a day. Frozen, canned and dried fruits and vegetables all count. Try to eat lots of different types. Add a portion or two of your favourite vegetables to your main meal.

Exercise burns up energy and can be a lot of fun!

Milk, cheese and yoghurt

Cheese is made from milk. It contains protein.

These cheeses have a creamy texture: cream cheese, fromage frais, ricotta, mozzarella

Soft cheese has a soft, sticky texture: Brie, Camembert

Hard cheese can be grated: Cheddar, Parmesan

Beware – some cheeses contain a lot of fat.

Food labels

Some foods are better for you than others. Foods that are high in salt, sugar or fat are not healthy if you eat them too often. Foods that are labelled 'low-fat' can sometimes contain a lot of sugar so it is a good idea to read the information on the packet carefully.

Choose wholegrain or wholewheat pasta and rice. They have lots of **vitamins**, **minerals** and **fibre**. They also taste great.

Look at the labels on food to find out which are high in salt, sugar and fat.

Shopping and planning

Planning, preparing and cooking food for yourself, friends and family is good fun and you get to eat well too!

Think of something you would like to make for a main meal. Write a shopping list of the things you need.

Check with the people you are cooking for to find out if there are any foods they dislike. Some people do not eat meat or fish. They are called vegetarians.

Before you start cooking, read through the recipe and collect all the ingredients and equipment together.

Cooking

Read the instructions carefully before you start. Ask an adult to explain anything that you do not understand.

A tidy kitchen is much easier to work in than a messy one. Tidy up and put things away as you work.

Wash the dishes and wipe down work surfaces as you prepare and cook the food.

Chicken to dip

These tasty nuggets of chicken are perfect to eat with a sweet and spicy dip and crunchy salad.

You will need

- tablespoon
- bowl
- plate
- baking tray
- oven mitts or thick cloth
- small pot and serving plate

Ingredients

- 1 tablespoon oil
- 2 tablespoons stuffing mix
- 2 tablespoons plain flour
- 2 tablespoons grated Cheddar cheese (see page 29)
- 225 g (8 oz) chicken mini fillets or sliced chicken breast
- 2 tablespoons sweet chilli sauce
- 4 tablespoons mayonnaise
- cherry tomatoes, sticks of cucumber and peppers

This makes enough for 2 people.

Before you start

- Preheat the oven to 200°C (400°F).

1

- Measure the oil into a bowl.

2

- Put the stuffing mix, flour and grated cheese on to a plate.
- Mix together.

3

- Dip one of the chicken pieces in the oil until it is covered all over.

- Roll the chicken piece in the flour, cheese and stuffing mix.

- Place the chicken piece on the baking tray. Repeat stages 3 and 4 with the rest of the chicken pieces.

- Cook in the oven for 15 to 20 minutes.
- Using the oven mitts or cloth, take out the baking tray.
- Ask an adult to check that the chicken is cooked properly.
- Turn off the oven.

- Mix the sweet chilli sauce and mayonnaise in a bowl.

Serve some dipping sauce in a pot with the chicken pieces, cucumber, peppers and tomatoes round it.

Get dipping!

| 45 minutes |
| Medium |
| Cooked |

These tasty burgers are made with the cheese in the middle. Open them up for a cheesy surprise.

You will need

- 1 large mixing bowl
- wooden spoon
- 1 small mixing bowl
- fork
- chopping board
- small knife

Ingredients

- 225 g (8 oz) minced beef
- 1 egg
- 50 g (2 oz) Cheddar cheese
- 1 onion, peeled and chopped
- 2 teaspoons dried mixed herbs
- a pinch of salt
- salad to serve with the burgers (see pages 14–15)

This makes 4 burgers.

Before you start

- Turn the **grill** on to high.

1
- Put the minced beef in the large mixing bowl. Break up any lumps with a wooden spoon.

2
- Crack the egg (see page 28) into the small mixing bowl and whisk with a fork.

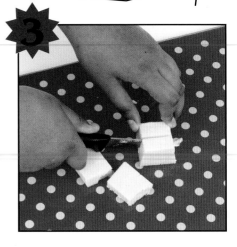

3
- Cut the cheese into four pieces.

- Put the egg, onion and mixed herbs into the bowl with the meat. Add the salt and mix everything together.
- Tip the mixture on to the chopping board.

- Divide the mixture into four and shape each piece into a ball.
- Flatten each ball with your hand to make your burgers.

- Put a piece of cheese in the middle of each burger.
- Wrap the meat round the cheese. There should not be any cheese showing.

- Put the burgers into a grill pan. Grill for about 8 minutes on each side.
- Ask an adult to check that the burgers are cooked properly.
- Turn off the grill.

Serve each burger with a delicious salad.

Mmmmm

30 minutes

Medium

Cooked

stuffed potato skins

Potatoes make a filling base for a main meal. Use these fillings or experiment with some of your own.

Ingredients

- 2 medium baking potatoes (washed)
- 1 tablespoon vegetable oil
- small tin of tuna fish (drained)
- 2 tablespoons soured cream
- 2 tablespoons sweetcorn
- 2 spring onions, finely chopped
- 2 tablespoons grated Cheddar cheese

You will need

- baking tray
- fork
- pastry brush
- sharp knife
- tablespoon
- mixing bowl
- potato masher

Before you start

- Preheat the oven to 190°C (375°F).

1

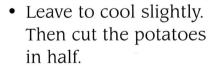

- Put the potatoes on the baking tray. Prick the potatoes all over with a fork.
- Brush with the oil.
- Cook for an hour or until they are soft.

2

- Leave to cool slightly. Then cut the potatoes in half.

3

- Scoop the soft potato into the mixing bowl. (Be careful not to break the skins.)
- Mash the potato (see page 29).

- Mix the tuna fish, soured cream and sweetcorn with the potato.

- Pile the mixture back into the skins.
- Top each potato with a few chopped spring onions.

- Put the potatoes back into the (cooled) baking tray.
- Top each one with a quarter of the grated cheese.
- Put into the oven until the cheese is melted and golden brown.
- Turn off the oven.

Delicious

Suggestion

Instead of a baking potato, use a large sweet potato. Mix the sweet potato with a tablespoon of soured cream and a quarter teaspoon of nutmeg. Top with grated cheese.

1 ½ hours

Medium

Cooked

13

'Filling' salads

Choose chunky potato, pasta or rice. Add some extras from the list below and make your perfect salad.

Ingredients

Salad base
Either:
- 225 g (8 oz) small new potatoes
- 2 tablespoons mayonnaise

or
- 115 g (4 oz) dried pasta
- 2 tablespoons mayonnaise

or
- 115 g (4 oz) brown rice
- salad dressing (see Handy hint)

Plus anything from this list:
- sausages – cooked and sliced
- ham – cooked and cut into small pieces
- tuna fish – drained and broken up
- chicken – cooked and cut into small pieces
- prawns – cooked
- tinned sweetcorn – drained
- peas – cooked
- green beans – cooked and chopped
- salmon – cooked and flaked
- broccoli cooked and cut into small pieces

Potatoes
- Put them in a saucepan. Cover them in water and bring to the boil. Cook for 20 to 30 minutes. Turn off the hob.
- Drain in a colander.
- Leave to cool.
- Cut into halves, or quarters if they are large.

Handy hint!

To make a creamy salad dressing, mix a tablespoon of creme fraiche with a few chopped chives and a squirt of lemon juice.

Rice

- Put the rice in a saucepan. Cover it in water and bring to the boil. Cook for 20 to 30 minutes. Turn off the hob.
- Ask an adult to drain the rice into the sieve (over a sink).
- Leave to cool.

Pasta

- Put the pasta in a saucepan. Cover it in water and bring to the boil. Cook for the time stated on the packet. Turn off the hob.
- Ask an adult to drain the pasta in a colander (over a sink).
- Leave to cool.

- **Either** mix the potato or pasta with the mayonnaise **or** mix the rice with the salad dressing.

- Add your choice of extra ingredients and mix together.

Sausage and prawn pasta salad

Mixed vegetable potato salad

Salmon and vegetable rice salad

| 40 minutes |
| Easy |
| Cooked |

Macaroni cheese

Creamy macaroni cheese is always a favourite. Add a portion of green vegetables for a healthy, balanced meal.

Pasta
Pasta is a starchy food (see page 4). It gives you energy. Wholewheat pasta is made from wheat that has not had the outer bran layer removed to make it white. As well as having more flavour, wholewheat pasta contains more vitamins, minerals and fibre than white pasta.

Ingredients

- 30 g (1 oz) butter
- 1 tablespoon plain flour
- 300 ml (10 fl oz) milk
- 50 g (2 oz) grated Cheddar cheese
- 100 g (3½ oz) macaroni, cooked and drained
- vegetables and crusty bread

You will need

- saucepan
- wooden spoon
- measuring jug
- whisk
- mixing spoon
- baking dish

Before you start

- Turn the hob on to medium.

1

- Melt the butter in the saucepan.

2

- Add the flour and milk.

3

- Whisk everything together until it is thick and smooth.

16

4

- Add half the cheese. Whisk again until smooth.

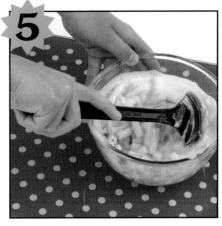

5

- Mix the sauce and cooked macaroni together.

6

- Tip the macaroni and sauce into a baking dish.
- Top with the rest of the grated cheese.
- Turn the grill on to high.

7

- Put the dish under a hot grill for a few minutes until the cheese is melted and golden brown.
- Turn off grill.

Serve with the vegetables and some crusty bread.

Cheesylicious!

| 40 minutes |
| Medium |
| Cooked |

Cheesy beans

Beans on toast make an easy and filling snack meal. Add some cheese and a portion of mushrooms to make it even more delicious.

Ingredients

- 1 medium-sized mushroom
- 1 teaspoon cooking oil
- portion baked beans
- slice wholemeal bread, toasted and buttered
- grated cheese

You will need

- small saucepan
- spoon
- small sharp knife
- chopping board
- small frying pan
- fish slice
- serving spoon
- plate

Beans

Baked beans are **pulses**. They are a starchy food that contains fibre and protein. They are a good source of protein for people who do not eat meat. Three heaped tablespoons of pulses also count as one of your 5-a-day.

Before you start

- Turn the hob on to low.

1

- Slice the mushroom.

2

- Put the oil into the frying pan. Add the mushrooms and cook until they are soft.
- Turn off the hob.

18

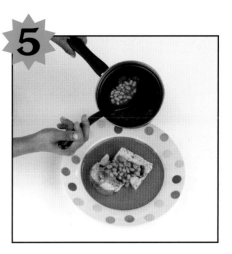

- Empty the beans into the saucepan.
- Put on to the hob and heat gently.

- Spoon the mushrooms on to the buttered toast.

- Top with the beans.

Yummmm

- Finish with a sprinkle of grated cheese.

15 minutes

Easy

Cooked

19

Creamy salmon
and vegetable pasta

This creamy pasta supper dish is as quick to make as any ready-meal. It is tasty and healthy, too.

You will need

- frying pan
- fish slice
- plate
- large saucepan
- sieve or colander
- grater
- fork
- mixing spoon

Fish

A healthy diet includes at least two portions of fish a week, including one of **oily fish**.

Oily fish – salmon, mackerel, sardines, trout and herring

White fish – haddock, plaice, pollack, coley and cod

Shellfish – prawns, mussels and lobster

Ingredients

- 30 g (1 oz) butter
- 2 salmon fillets
- 125 g (4½ oz) fresh pasta
- 1 lemon
- 115 g (4 oz) green vegetables, cooked and cut into pieces
- 2 tablespoons creme fraiche

This makes enough for 2 people.

- Turn the hob to medium and melt the butter in the frying saucepan.

- Add the fish and cook for 4 minutes.
- Using the fish slice, turn it over and cook for another 4 minutes.

- Take the fish out and put it on to a plate.
- Turn the hob to high.
- Half-fill the large saucepan with water and put it on the hob.

4

- When the water is hot add the pasta. Bring the water to the boil and cook for 4 minutes.
- Ask an adult to drain the pasta into the sieve or colander (over a sink).

5

- Put the drained pasta back in the saucepan.
- Turn the hob down to low.
- Grate the yellow skin (rind) from the lemon into the saucepan.

6

- Break the fish into small pieces with a fork. Add the fish to the saucepan.

7

- Add the cooked vegetables and creme fraiche.
- Put the saucepan back on the hob and heat very gently for a minute or two.
- Turn off the hob.

Wow!

| 15 minutes |
| Medium |
| Cooked |

Sticky chicken

These sticky chicken drumsticks are coated with a barbecue-flavour sauce. They are a perfect summer picnic dish.

You will need

- tablespoon
- saucepan
- wooden spoon
- baking tray
- oven mitts
- kitchen foil

Before you start

- Turn the hob to medium.
- Turn the oven to 200°C (400°F).

Ingredients

- 4 chicken drumsticks

For the sauce:
- 1 tablespoon sunflower oil or olive oil
- 2 tablespoons tomato ketchup
- 1 tablespoon soy sauce
- 1 tablespoon clear honey

To serve:
- 2 portions rice salad made with peas, green beans and sweetcorn (see page 15)

This makes enough for 2 people.

1

- Measure all the sauce ingredients into the saucepan.

2

- Put the pan on the hob.
- Melt the ingredients together. Stir with a wooden spoon. When they are mixed, turn off the hob.

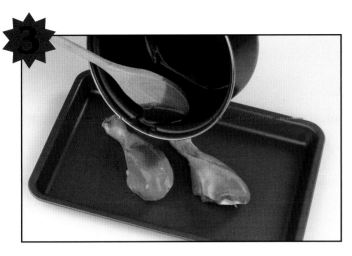

- Put the chicken drumsticks on to a baking tray.
- Pour the sauce over them.

- Cook in the oven for 15 minutes.
- Using the oven mitts, take out the tray. Spoon the sauce back over the chicken.
- Put the drumsticks back in the oven and cook for a further 15 minutes.
- Ask an adult to check that the chicken is cooked properly.
- Wrap foil round the ends of the drumsticks to make them easier to pick up.
- Turn off the oven.

Serve with a rice salad (see page 15).

Stickylicious!

| 40 minutes |
| Medium |
| Cooked |

squidgy meringues

These 'light as a feather' meringues are very easy to make, and melt in the mouth.

Ingredients

- 2 eggs, separated (see page 28)
- 115 g (4 oz) **caster sugar**
- double cream, whipped (see page 29)
- raspberries

You will need

- large mixing bowl
- electric whisk
- baking tray
- dessertspoon
- kitchen knife

Handy hint!

It is very important not to get any yolk in the egg white when you separate the eggs. If you do, the egg whites will not thicken.

1

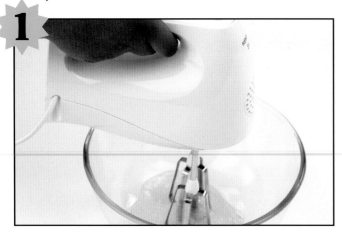

- Put the egg whites into a bowl.
- Whisk with the electric whisk on fast until the whites are very thick. To check – turn off the whisk. Lift it out of the mixture. The egg whites should stand up in stiff points.
- Whisk in the sugar a bit at a time.

2

- Put spoonfuls of the mixture on to a baking tray.
- Turn the oven to 120°C (250°F).
- **Bake** the meringues for one-and-a-half to two hours. They should be firm and dry to touch.

- Turn off the oven and leave the meringues to cool.
- When they are cold, spread the bases with a blob of whipped cream.

- Sandwich the meringues together.
- Decorate with raspberries.

Yummmm

| 2-3 hours |
| Tricky |
| Cooked |

Special fruit kebabs

These fruit kebabs with a chocolate coating are a great way to add to your 5-a-day (see page 5).

You will need

- mixing bowl
- saucepan
- 4 wooden kebab skewers
- small knife
- cooling rack

Ingredients

- small bar milk or plain chocolate
- 8 strawberries
- 8 grapes
- 8 marshmallows
- 8 pieces of pineapple

This makes 4 kebabs.

1

- Break the chocolate into the mixing bowl.
- Turn the hob on to medium.

2

- Put some water in the pan. Rest the bowl on top of the pan. The water should not touch the bottom of the bowl.

3

- Put the pan on the hob. Stir occasionally as the chocolate melts.

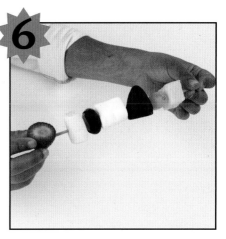

- When the chocolate has melted, take the pan off the heat.
- Turn off the hob.
- Using one of the wooden skewers, dip some of the fruits and marshmallows into the melted chocolate.

- Leave the chocolate-covered fruits and marshmallows on the cooling rack to set.

- Thread the fruit and marshmallows on to the skewers. Push the skewers through the parts not covered in chocolate.

Scrummy

1 hour

Easy

Uncooked

How to!

Crack open an egg

- Tap the egg gently on the side of a bowl so that it cracks.

- Put your two thumbs on either side of the crack.

- Hold the egg over the bowl and gently pull the shell apart.

Separate an egg

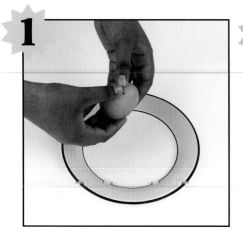

- Break the egg on to a plate.

- Place an egg cup over the egg yolk.

- Hold the egg cup in place and tip the egg white into a bowl.

Grate

A food grater has lots of sharp blades that can turn food into strips.

A box grater has different-sized blades for different foods.

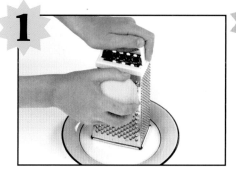

- The finest blades are for grating the rind of oranges and lemons.

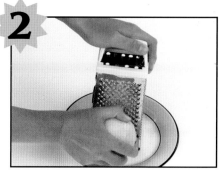

- Hold the top of the grater to stop it slipping.
- Press food against the blades and push down.
- Mind your fingers.

Whisk or whip

To whisk or whip means to stir quickly to add air to a liquid. Double or whipping cream is whipped to make it thick.

A whisk is a kitchen utensil designed for whisking liquids (see page 31).

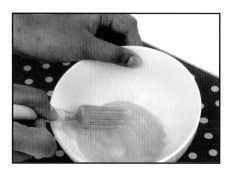

- This egg yolk is being whisked with a fork.

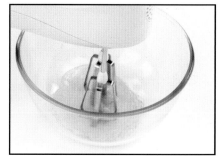

- Whisking egg whites is much quicker using an electric whisk.

Mash

A potato masher is used to mash food. It has holes in it that the food is pushed through to break it up.

A fork can be used to mash soft foods such as bananas.

- Potatoes are usually mashed with a potato masher.

- This banana is being mashed with a fork.

Glossary

artificial colouring A manufactured colouring added to food.

artificial flavouring Manufactured flavours that are added to food.

bake To cook in an oven with heat all round the food.

caster sugar A type of very fine white sugar with small grains.

energy A type of power that can be used. Food is changed to energy in our body.

exercise Physical activity that uses up calories (energy) and improves fitness.

fat 1. A greasy substance found in food. Fats in food are divided into two types: **saturated fats** are found in cream, cheese, butter, suet, lard, fatty meat and chocolate; **unsaturated fats** are found in avocados, nuts, vegetable oils and olive oils. Unsaturated fats are healthier than saturated fats.
2. Tissue in the human body where energy is stored.

fibre The part of a fruit or vegetable that cannot be digested. Fibre helps the digestion of other food.

grill A way of cooking food using direct heat from above or below.

mineral A substance such as iron or calcium that the body needs to function properly. Minerals are found in foods.

oily fish Fish that have oily flesh. These fish contain substances that help to prevent heart disease.

preservative A substance used to stop food going bad.

processed food Any food product that has been changed in some way. Cooking, freezing, drying, canning and preserving are all methods of processing food. Processed foods may contain colourings, flavourings and other additives and preservatives.

protein A substance found in some foods. It is needed by the body to grow and develop properly. Meat, eggs, milk and some types of beans contain protein.

pulse One of various edible seeds, such as peas, beans and lentils.

starchy Describes a food that contains starch. Starchy foods make up one of the food groups. They include bread, cereals, rice, pasta and potatoes.

vitamin One of the substances that are essential in very small amounts in the body for normal growth and activity.

wholegrain Cereals such as wheat, barley and oats that have not had the outer layer taken off.

wholewheat The entire grain of wheat including the outer layer (bran).

vegetarian Someone who eats no meat or fish. Some vegetarians do eat dairy foods and eggs.

Equipment

wire cooling rack

sieve

cutting board

pastry brush

measuring jug

fish slice

mixing bowl

grater

mixing or serving spoon

whisk

tablespoon

dessertspoon

teaspoon

saucepan

knife

small sharp knife

frying pan

You will also need:
tea-towel
weighing scales
oven gloves
kitchen foil
electric whisk
baking dish
wooden skewers

wooden spoons

colander

non-stick baking tray

Index

Activity sheets

The following pages have accompanying sheets which are available to download for free at www.franklinwatts.co.uk.

Pages 4–5 All about main meals
Plan your main meals for the week ahead on this handy food chart. Fill in the shopping list so you know what you need to buy.

Pages 6–7 All about main meals
What main meals do your friends like best? Fill in this food survey to find out which are the most popular.

Page 31 Equipment
Download a colourful poster of all the equipment used in the 'Plan Prepare Cook' books.